Orthodox Answers to
Frequently Asked Questions

Thorough and biblical answers
to eight of the most common questions
Protestants ask about the Orthodox Church
presented in a simple and
straightforward outline form

By Father Marc Dunaway

CONCILIAR PRESS
Ben Lomond, California

Printed in Canada

Orthodox Answers to Frequently Asked Questions
© Copyright 2002 by Marc Dunaway

All Rights Reserved

Published by Conciliar Press
P.O. Box 76
Ben Lomond, California 95005-0076

ISBN 1-888212-62-4

Unless otherwise noted, all Scripture quotations are from
the New King James Version of the Bible, © 1982
by Thomas Nelson, Inc., Nashville, Tennessee
and are used by permission.

CONTENTS

1. Why Honor Mary? .... page 5

2. Why "Ever-Virgin"? .... page 9

3. Why "Father"? .... page 14

4. Why Incense? .... page 17

5. Why the Sign of the Cross? .... page 21

6. Why Tradition? .... page 25

7. Why Icons? .... page 29

8. Why "Organized" Church? .... page 35

Q. Why is it proper to honor Mary?

A. To begin with, the Bible shows us that it is. Beyond this there are two basic reasons why it is proper to honor her:
1. because she is the mother of Jesus Christ, our Lord and God;
2. because she is a model of obedient submission to God.

Honoring Mary does not mean we "worship" her.

I. The Bible shows us that it is proper to honor Mary.

A. **The angel Gabriel honored Mary** when he came to announce that she would bear a Son: "And having come in, the angel said to her, '**Rejoice, highly favored** *one,* the Lord *is* with you; **blessed** [Greek *eulogeméne,* 'speak well of, praise'] *are* **you among women!**'" (Luke 1:28).

B. **God honored Mary.** Gabriel said, "Do not be afraid, Mary, for **you have found favor with God**" (Luke 1:30).

C. **Elizabeth, the mother of John the Baptist, honored Mary.** When Mary went to visit Elizabeth, Elizabeth greeted her, saying: "**Blessed** [Greek *eulogeméne*] *are* **you among women,** and blessed *is* the fruit of your womb! But **why** *is* this *granted* **to me, that the mother of my Lord should come to me?**" (Luke 1:42, 43).

D. **Mary herself prophesied:** ". . . henceforth all generations will call me blessed [Greek *makariousîn,* 'call happy or blessed']" (Luke 1:48). (All generations, it seems, except the present generation of some Protestants.)

E. **Jesus honored Mary.** We can be sure of this because He obeyed the Ten Commandments perfectly, the fifth commandment being, "You shall honor your father and your mother."

Conclusion: If Mary was held in honor by God, by Gabriel, by Elizabeth, and by our Lord Himself, then those who follow Him should do likewise. If not, they may have to answer to Him for it someday.

II. We honor Mary because she is the Mother of Jesus Christ, our Lord and God.

A. **Mary was specially chosen** and prepared by God to fulfill this task. She had a holiness and spirituality that made her pleasing to God. She was not just "in the right place at the right time."

B. **Because of this she holds a special place in our salvation** as the means through which the Son of God came into our world as a man.

C. **This was a very great honor that remains uniquely hers forever.** This is why the Church calls her "more honorable than the cherubim and more glorious beyond compare than the seraphim."

D. **The terms "Mother of God" and "God-bearer"** [Greek *Theotokos*] **are also proper titles for Mary.**

   1. These terms have been especially crucial to the Church ever since the fifth century when it was faced with the attack of a heretic named Nestorius.

   2. These terms were not originally employed in order to exalt Mary, but rather to exalt Christ and to protect the true Christian belief about Him.

   3. If Christ was truly God and if Mary was Christ's mother, then it follows that she can rightly be called the Mother of God or the God-bearer.
      a. This does not mean that she had anything to do with His eternal existence as God or with originating His divinity.
      b. It means that the very same person she gave birth to in Bethlehem 2000 years ago was also the eternal Son of God who existed before all ages.
      c. It means that noone can say, as Nestorius was attempting to say, that Jesus—who was Mary's son and God's eternal Son—was really two different persons.

4. Referring to Mary as the "Mother of God" protects and preserves the mystery of the Incarnation. As such, then, it is not an optional title of devotion, but a dogma that lies at the very heart of the Christian faith.

Conclusion: Because of Mary's special role in our salvation as the mother of our Lord and God, Jesus Christ, all Christians should give her due honor. Protestants need to understand the term "Mother of God" and confess her as such. Those who cannot or will not do so show that they may not understand who Jesus Christ truly is.

III. We honor Mary because she is a model of obedient submission to God.

A. Later in Jesus' ministry, a woman cried out to Him from a crowd, "Blessed *is* the womb that bore You, and *the* breasts which nursed You!" (Luke 11:27). But Jesus replied, "More than that, blessed *are* those who hear the word of God and keep it!" (v. 28). Jesus was not dishonoring His mother here. Rather, He was giving an even greater reason for honoring her, for **Mary was one who had heard the word of God and kept it.** Another legitimate translation of Jesus' reply could be: "Yes, indeed, blessed are those who hear the word of God and keep it." (Compare Romans 10:18 and Philippians 3:8 for other places where the Greek word *menounge* is translated "Yes, indeed.")

B. When Gabriel appeared to Mary and told her that she was to bear the Son of God, though troubled and unclear as to what all this would mean, she nevertheless replied: **"Behold the maidservant of the Lord! Let it be to me according to your word"** (Luke 1:38).

   1. Without this willing cooperation on the part of Mary, Christ could not have been born to save the world.

   2. But because of this obedient cooperation, Mary became a model and a picture of Christian submission and obedience to God.

   3. Moreover, Christ dwelling within her and being born from her became a picture of the fruit that can come from such cooperation with the will of God.

Conclusion: Because of Mary's special role in submitting to the will of God so that Christ could be born into the world, she has become a picture and a model for every Christian; for without such voluntary and humble submission to God, no one can bring forth fruits of righteousness. Many Christians would benefit by re-establishing Mary as a role model of the faith in place of some of the teenage idols and Hollywood stars that they and their children put on pedestals and posters.

IV. Honoring Mary does not mean we "worship" her.

A. Worship belongs to God alone.

B. The honor shown to Mary means we give her special esteem and hold her in high regard above all others.

   1. The Orthodox Church has always been careful to maintain this distinction. The Church uses the Greek word *latreia* to define the worship reserved for God alone and *douleia* for the honor proper to Mary and other saints.

   2. In English, we can show this distinction by distinguishing between the words "worship" and "honor," or "worship" and "veneration."

C. **Many Protestants, though,** do not even honor Mary at all, but **have actually dishonored her by ignoring her special place in the Church.**

   1. They have done this in reaction to what they have seen as abuses within the Roman Catholic Church.

   2. But in so doing they have "thrown the baby out with the bath water."

   3. The tradition of the Orthodox Church has remained free from these abuses. For example, Orthodox tradition does not hold to the doctrine of the Immaculate Conception of Mary as it was formulated by Pope Pius IX in 1854. (This teaches that Mary herself was conceived and born without original sin.)

Conclusion: Protestants need to stop dishonoring Mary and return to honoring her rightly. This will not rob God of worship; rather, it will bring Him greater glory by recognizing those whom He has glorified with His grace.

In summary, we can show that it is proper to honor Mary because this is consistent with certain examples in the Bible; because she is the Mother of our Lord; and because, through her humble cooperation and submission to the will of God, she became a fitting role model for all Christians to follow. Furthermore, Protestants need to realize that the terms "Mother of God" and "God-bearer," while honoring Mary, are meant foremost to exalt Christ and to protect the true belief about His Incarnation. Then they need to confess Mary as such and come in line with the long-standing belief and practice of the Church. Those who have dishonored Mary by ignoring her or even speaking ill of her need to repent and begin to honor her rightly in place of the godless role models that are exalted by our present culture, even in the homes of some Christians.

> *Q.* Why do we believe that Mary was "ever-virgin"?
>
> *A.* Because the tradition of the Church from its earliest days has always taught that Mary was ever-virgin and that she chose not to have any other children besides our Lord. There are verses from the Bible which some have taken to indicate that she did have other children, but it can be shown that these are not conclusive on the matter. This is not a matter of faith so much as part of the "family" tradition of the Church.

I. Throughout the writings of the Church Fathers from the fourth century on, Mary is consistently referred to as "ever-virgin."

   A. These include: Peter of Alexandria, Epiphanius, Athanasius, Didymus the Blind, Jerome, Cyril of Alexandria, Leo, Sophronius of Jerusalem, John of Damascus, and the capitula of the Second Council of Constantinople in A.D. 553.

   B. **Even the Protestant Reformers Martin Luther and John Calvin and the great Methodist leader John Wesley wrote and taught that Mary was ever-virgin.**

Conclusion: That Mary remained ever-virgin after giving birth to our Lord is part of the long-standing "family" tradition of the Church.

II. **We believe Mary remained ever-virgin because she understood the special honor and privilege given to her to bear the Son of God, and thereafter voluntarily chose to have no other children.**

A. Ambrose, bishop of Milan in the fourth century, wrote: "The virgin did not seek the consolation of bearing another child" (see Letter 63; *Nicene and Post-Nicene Fathers,* vol. 10, p. 473). Many other such quotes can be found also.

B. Martin Luther wrote: "Mary realized she was the Mother of the Son of God, and she did not desire to become the mother of the son of man, but to remain in this divine gift" (see *Mary in Protestant and Catholic Theology,* Thomas O'Meara, p. 120).

Conclusion: If those who doubt this will give due consideration to what Mary must have felt when she realized her special privilege, it will not seem surprising that she chose to have no other children.

III. The verses in the Bible that seem to indicate that Mary had other children are not conclusive on the matter.

A. "Joseph . . . took to him his wife, and did not know her **till she had brought forth her firstborn Son**" (Matthew 1:24, 25).

  1. The intent of this statement by Matthew was not to imply anything about the time after Jesus' birth, but simply to affirm the present virginity of Mary and the miraculous conception of her Child. It is hermeneutically unsound to use this passage to try to show that Mary was not ever-virgin. (See St. John Chrysostom's Homily 5 on the Gospel of Matthew, *Nicene and Post-Nicene Fathers,* vol. 10, p. 65.)

  2. **In modern English, the word "till" would seem to imply that Mary no longer remained a virgin after she gave birth to Jesus.** But *eos ou,* **the Greek word for "till" used here, does not necessarily mean this.** (See *Mary in the New Testament,* p. 86, nt. 177.)

  3. The word *eos ou,* **"till," is used elsewhere in the Scriptures to mean "always," and not to refer to some specific period of time.**
     a. For example, *eos ou* is translated as "even to" in Matthew 28:20: " . . . and lo, I am with you always, ***even to*** the end of the age." Yet it would be ridiculous to assume from this that after the end of the age Jesus would no longer be with His disciples.
     b. Therefore, Matthew 1:25 could justifiably read, "Joseph . . . did not know her *even up to* the time she brought forth her firstborn Son."
     c. Other verses where "until" implies "always" are: Genesis 28:15; Psalm 110:1; John 9:18; and 1 Timothy 4:13.

B. "A multitude was sitting around Him; and they said to Him, 'Look, Your mother **and Your brothers** are outside seeking You'" (Mark 3:32). "'Is this not the carpenter, the Son of Mary, and **brother of James, Joses, Judas, and Simon?**'" (Mark 6:3). [Parallel passages appear in Matthew 12:47 and 13:55 as well as Luke 8:20.]

1. Though these men are called Jesus' "brothers," this verse does not state, nor does any other in the Bible, that they are specifically sons of Mary, the Lord's mother.

2. In the Aramaic language used at that time, the word "brother" was also used to describe cousins or other close relatives. The same is true of the Greek word for brother, *adelphos*.
   a. Right in the same context, in fact, our Lord goes on to make this statement, "Whoever does the will of God is My brother and My sister and mother" (Mark 3:35).
   b. In his letter to the Romans, St. Paul uses the same Greek word, *adelphos*, writing, "my brethren, my countrymen according to the flesh" (Romans 9:3).
   c. Such a broad use of the word "brother" is not even unfamiliar today, as in "soul-brother" or the International Brotherhood of Electrical Workers (IBEW).
   d. In Genesis 29:12 (KJV), Jacob calls himself Laban's "brother" (the Septuagint [LXX] uses the word *adelphos*) when, in fact, Laban was his uncle.
   e. "It is well known that in the New Testament *adelphos* at times denotes other relationships [besides blood brother]" (*Mary in the New Testament*, p. 65).

3. In the tradition of the Church, these "brothers" of Jesus have been identified as **other relatives of Jesus living with Mary** for one reason or another.
   a. They could be **the children of Joseph by a previous marriage** and therefore Jesus' stepbrothers.
   b. They could be **the children of either Mary's or Joseph's sister**, who somehow came under the care of Joseph's family, and therefore were His cousins.

Conclusion: Nowhere in the Bible is it specifically stated that Mary did not remain a virgin after Christ's birth or that she had other children. The exact relationship between Jesus and His "brothers" cannot be determined conclusively from the Bible; but it can be shown that "brother" here does not necessarily have to mean the son of the same mother.

IV. There are other passages in the Bible that seem to indicate that Mary did *not* have other children and that the "brothers" of the Lord were not her sons.

A. In the accounts of the crucifixion that appear in the Gospels, the following women are mentioned as being present.

Mark 15:40	Matthew 27:56	John 19:25
Mary Magdalene	Mary Magdalene	Mary Magdalene
Salome	The mother of the sons of Zebedee	Jesus' mother's sister
Mary the mother of James the Less and Joses	Mary the mother of James and Joses	Mary wife of Clopas
		Jesus' mother

1. Mary Magdalene is mentioned the same way in all three.

2. Church tradition identifies Salome, the mother of the sons of Zebedee (that is, James and John), and the sister of our Lord's mother to be one and the same person. (This means that the disciples James and John were the Lord's cousins.)

3. **Mary the mother of James and Joses could be identified with the Mary mentioned by John as Mary the wife of Clopas.** If this is true, and if James and Joses are the same as those mentioned above in Mark 6:3, then it would prove that James the Less and Joses were not sons of Mary, the Lord's mother, but relatives of Jesus in some other way. Such has been the most widely accepted view throughout church history.

B. The following incident is recorded at our Lord's crucifixion: "When Jesus therefore saw His mother, and the disciple whom He loved [John] standing by, He said to His mother, 'Woman, behold your son!' Then He said to the disciple, 'Behold your mother!' And from that hour that disciple took her to his own *home*" (John 19:26, 27). **If Mary had had other sons, the Lord would not have commended her into the care of His disciple John.** But since she did not, this was proper and necessary.

In summary to the question of proving Mary's ever-virginity, the book, *Mary in the New Testament,* a joint work of Catholic and Lutheran scholars published in 1978, offers these four points:
1. The continued virginity of Mary after the birth of Jesus is not a question directly raised by the New Testament.
2. Once it was raised in subsequent church history, it was that question which focused attention on the exact relationship of the "brothers" (and "sisters") to Jesus.

3. Once that attention has been focused, it cannot be said that the New Testament identifies them *without doubt* as blood brothers and sisters and hence as children of Mary.
4. The solution favored by scholars will in part depend on the authority they accord to later church insights.

Considering the above, especially the inconclusiveness of the Scriptures on the matter, *and* since it has been the consistent belief of the Church from its earliest centuries that Mary remained ever-virgin and had no children besides our Lord, one should ask, why would any Christian want to believe otherwise?

See also: Mary in the New Testament: A Collaborative Assessment by Protestant and Roman Catholic Scholars, *edited by Raymond Brown, Karl Donfried, Joseph Fitzmyer, and John Reumann; 1978, Fortress Press, Philadelphia, and Paulist Press, New York.*

> *Q.* Why do we call our priests "father," when Jesus said in Matthew 23:9, "Do not call anyone on earth your father"?
>
> *A.* Our Lord was not speaking literally in Matthew 23:9; rather the context shows that His true aim was to put down the pride and arrogance of the scribes and Pharisees.

I. Our Lord was not speaking literally in Matthew 23:9.

A. If the statement, "Do not call *anyone* on earth your father," is to be taken literally, it would mean that natural fathers or the founders of cities or countries should not be called "father" either. But all Christians without reservation call their natural fathers "father" and George Washington the "father" of the United States. This shows that this statement cannot be taken literally, but must be interpreted.

B. Many times in the Bible men are called "father."

1. **2 Kings 2:12**—When Elijah was taken to heaven in a chariot of fire, his follower Elisha cried out: **"My father, my father . . ."**

2. **Luke 16:24, 25**—Our Lord, in telling the parable about the rich man and Lazarus, put these words into the mouth of the rich man: "**Father Abraham**, have mercy on me." Abraham did not reply, "Don't you know that no man on earth is to be called 'father'?" No, he said: "Son, remember . . ."

3. **Acts 7:2**—Stephen addressed the court of the high priest, saying: "Brethren and **fathers**, listen . . ."

4. **Acts 22:1**—Paul began his address to a mob in Jerusalem by saying: "Brethren and **fathers**, hear my defense . . ."

5. **1 Corinthians 4:15**—Paul referred to himself as *the spiritual father of the church in Corinth*: "For though you might have ten thousand instructors in Christ, yet *you do* not *have* many fathers; for in Christ Jesus **I have begotten you** through the gospel."

6. **1 Corinthians 10:1**—Paul called his spiritual ancestors "fathers": "Moreover, brethren, I do not want you to be unaware that all **our fathers** were under the cloud . . ."

7. **Ephesians 6:4** and **Colossians 3:21**—Paul addressed natural fathers, saying: "**Fathers**, do not provoke your children . . ."

C. **If Matthew 23:9 is to be taken literally, then so should Matthew 23:10 (or Matthew 23:8), which reads, "Do not be called teachers." Yet often the same Christians who believe they should not call anyone "father" will not hesitate to call someone "teacher."** Some Protestant pastors are even officially called "Doctor," which is simply the Latin word for "teacher." If this is permissible, then it should also be appropriate to call a pastor or a priest "father" in the right way.

Conclusion: The normal usage of the terms "father" and "teacher" makes it clear that our Lord did not mean us to take His statement in Matthew 23:9 in the wooden, literal sense. Moreover, we should not think we know more about what Jesus meant than did St. Paul, who himself did not hesitate to use the term "father" appropriately.

II. The context of the statement in Matthew 23:9 shows that our Lord's true aim was to put down the pride and arrogance of the scribes and Pharisees.

A. Jesus described the attitude of the scribes and Pharisees, to whom He was referring, in this way:

1. Matthew 23:5—"all their works they do to be seen by men."

2. Matthew 23:5—"They make their phylacteries [i.e. small, leather cases holding slips inscribed with Scripture passages, fastened with leather thongs to the forehead and the left arm] broad and enlarge the borders of their garments."

3. Matthew 23:6—"They love the best places at feasts, the best seats in the synagogues . . ."

4. Matthew 23:7—"[They love] greetings in the marketplaces . . ."

5. Matthew 23:7—"[They love] to be called by men, 'Rabbi, Rabbi.'"

B. It is in response to this proud attitude that our Lord then said: "But you, do not be called 'Rabbi'; for One is your Teacher, the Christ, and you are all brethren. Do not call anyone on earth your father; for One is your Father, He who is in heaven. And do not be called teachers; for One is your Teacher, the Christ" (Matthew 23:8–10).

C. Philip Schaff, the famous Protestant scholar of the nineteenth century, commented on Matthew 23:9 this way: "It is plain, therefore, that the Savior prohibits not so much the titles themselves, as the spirit of pride and ambition which covets and abuses them, the *haughty* spirit which would domineer over inferiors, and also the *servile* spirit which would basely cringe to superiors" (*Lange's Commentary on the Holy Scriptures*, vol. 8, p. 410).

Conclusion: Our Lord spoke of Christian humility by saying: "But he who is greatest among you shall be your servant. And whoever exalts himself will be abased, and he who humbles himself will be exalted" (Matthew 23:11, 12). Here He showed how He meant His words to be understood and interpreted.

In summary, we can say that it is clear our Lord's words in Matthew 23:9 were not meant to be taken strictly and literally, but rather as a condemnation of pride and as an encouragement toward Christian humility. It is in this spirit, then, that the Church has followed the example of St. Paul (and others) and has not hesitated to call those who are spiritual fathers "father." **This is not a title of exaltation, but simply an expression of warmth and dignity, recognizing that those so called are properly imitating and mirroring the true Fatherhood of God, from whom come all good things.**

> ***Q.*** Why do we use incense in our worship?
>
> ***A.*** Incense is part of the joy and beauty of Orthodox worship. It is a symbol of our prayers ascending to God and of His transforming power in our lives. Furthermore, there is a great deal of biblical support for its place in worship, both in the Old and New Testaments.

I. Incense is part of the joy and beauty of Orthodox worship.

   A. Physical symbols are an important part of Orthodox worship.

      1. Everything God made is "good" (Genesis 1:31). The physical aspects of creation were meant to express the glory of God. Why shouldn't this also include the resinous sap of the Boswellia tree (native to North Africa and India) which can be used to give a sweet and symbolic fragrance to the offering of worship?

      2. Other physical aspects of worship common to nearly every Christian tradition include bowing the head, kneeling, praying with hands uplifted, etc.

      3. Other physical elements used in Christian worship include water in Baptism and bread and wine in the Lord's Supper or Eucharist.

      4. **Incense becomes a physical reminder of the special purpose at hand when we come to the church.** Simply put, when an Orthodox Christian

smells incense, no matter where he is or what he is doing, he thinks one thing—worship.

B. To those who ask, "**Is incense 'necessary' to worship?**" we respond: **Of course not. But who wants to settle in life for what is "necessary"?** Singing isn't "necessary" to worship either, but because it expresses the emotion of the heart in such a beautiful way, all Christians eagerly employ it in their worship. The same principle can apply to incense.

Conclusion: Why do we use incense? The best answer might simply be: We use incense because it smells good, and therefore we use it as an expression of beauty, of joy, and of our love for the Kingdom of God.

II. Incense is a symbol of our prayers ascending to God and of His transforming power in our lives.

A. **Incense is a picture of our prayers rising up to God.**

1. In Psalm 141:2, a psalm which is sung every evening in the Orthodox Vespers service, David says: **"Let my prayer be set before You as incense."**

2. John the Apostle, describing what he saw in his vision of heaven, refers in Revelation 5:8 to **"golden bowls full of incense, which are the prayers of the saints."**

3. In the services of preparation before the Divine Liturgy, the deacon brings the censer to the priest, who blesses the incense, saying, "We offer incense to you as a perfume of spiritual fragrance."

B. **Incense is also a picture of the transformation within a Christian when he is joined to the glowing radiance of God's power in Jesus Christ**, just like the resinous incense is transformed into a sweet fragrance when it is placed on the glowing coal in the censer.

1. Censing is done in the church as an act of preparation and sanctification. It shows the special, "transformed" purpose for which the people, the building, the altar, etc. have been set aside.

2. Censing the icons, the Gospel, the Gifts, or the people is also an act of sacred respect.

III. There is a great deal of biblical support for the use of incense in worship.

A. **Incense was an important part of the worship in the Old Testament.**
   1. The first mention of incense in the Bible is in Exodus 25:6, where God listed it among the offerings He sought from the children of Israel.
   2. A few chapters later, in Exodus 30, God gave Moses detailed descriptions for building the altar of incense in the tabernacle and careful instructions on how to make the proper kind of incense.
      a. "**You shall make an altar to burn incense on**; you shall make it of acacia wood." (Exodus 30:1).
      b. "And the LORD said to Moses: 'Take sweet spices, stacte and onycha and galbanum, and pure frankincense with these sweet spices; there shall be equal amounts of each. **You shall make of these an incense**, a compound according to the art of the perfumer, salted, pure, *and* holy'" (Exodus 30:34, 35).
      c. "... **the incense which you shall make ... shall be to you holy for the LORD.** Whoever makes *any* like it, to smell it, he shall be cut off from his people" (Exodus 30:37, 38).
   3. Later, God became angry with Israel because they offered incense wrongly and to foreign gods (see, for example, 2 Chronicles 34:25 and Jeremiah 11:12–17). But incense was still to remain an important part of their worship if used according to God's commandment.
   4. The last place incense is mentioned in the Old Testament is by the prophet Malachi: "'For from the rising of the sun, / Even to its going down, / My name *shall be* great among the Gentiles; / **In every place incense *shall be* offered to My name,** / And a pure offering; / For My name shall be great among the nations,' / Says the LORD of hosts" (Malachi 1:11). Many early Church Fathers (including Irenaeus, Justin Martyr, and Hippolytus, all men from the second and third centuries) saw the fulfillment of this prophecy in the eucharistic worship of the Church.

B. In the New Testament, Luke tells us that **Zacharias was offering incense in the Temple when the angel of the Lord appeared to him** to announce that Elizabeth would bear him a son (John the Baptist). Luke even describes where the angel stood: "An angel of the Lord appeared to him, standing on the right side of the altar of incense" (Luke 1:11).

C. **The wise men who traveled from the East to see the newborn Christ fell down and worshipped Him, and offered gifts of "gold, frankincense, and myrrh"** (Matthew 2:11). [In the Persian culture of that time, incense was reserved as a gift offered *only* to kings.]

D. Finally, incense is mentioned several times in the Book of Revelation as being present in heaven.

   1. "Now when He had taken the scroll, the four living creatures and the twenty-four elders fell down before the Lamb, each having a harp, and **golden bowls full of incense, which are the prayers of the saints**" (Revelation 5:8).

   2. "Then another angel, having a golden censer, came and stood at the altar. He was given much incense, that he should offer *it* with the prayers of all the saints upon the golden altar which was before the throne. And **the smoke of the incense, with the prayers of the saints, ascended before God from the angel's hand**" (Revelation 8:3, 4).

E. **Incense was not commonly used by the Church during the first three centuries.** This was because offering incense to the image of the Roman emperor was the basic test by which Christians were asked to renounce their faith and accept pagan worship. It was, therefore, naturally repugnant to them. **When the era of persecutions ended**, however, and with it the pagan Roman worship, **the Church soon began to reintroduce incense into its own worship in a proper way.**

Conclusion: Nowhere in the Bible is there a verse that says anything against incense used in the proper worship of God. On the contrary, incense is consistently mentioned as being part of the worship, whether it is in the tabernacle in the desert or among the angels in heaven. Certainly, then, it is appropriate that it has found a place in the tradition of Orthodox Christian worship.

In summary to the question of why we use incense in our worship, there are many points that could be brought forward in answer, some more convincing and important than others. But on the lighter side it might be best just to suggest this: Since St. John saw incense in heaven, doesn't it stand to reason we may as well get used to it here?

Q. Why do we make the sign of the cross?

A. This is one of the most ancient and universal traditions of the Church, which, although not specifically mentioned in the Bible, is certainly consonant with it. Christians have used this sign because the cross is the central symbol of the Christian Faith, and by tracing its shape upon ourselves we declare that we belong to Jesus Christ. Moreover, when accompanied by faith in Christ, this symbol can help us overcome the sinful passions of the body, the fear of death and the power of Satan.

I. Making the sign of the cross is an ancient and universal Christian custom.

   A. **Basil the Great**, writing around 370 A.D., made this very important statement: "If we attacked unwritten customs, claiming them to be of little importance, we would fatally mutilate the Gospel, no matter what our intentions—or rather, we would reduce the Gospel teaching to bare words. For instance (to take the first and most common example), where is the written teaching that we should sign with the sign of the Cross those who, trusting in the Name of Our Lord Jesus Christ, are to be enrolled as catechumens?" (*On the Holy Spirit*, ch. 27). [This custom of receiving the sign of the cross as a catechumen was then carried over into daily life by those who had been baptized.]

B. **Tertullian**, a Christian leader who died around A.D. 230, wrote: "In all our travels and movements, in all our coming in and going out, in putting on our shoes, at the bath, at the table, in lighting candles, in lying down, in sitting down, whatever employment occupies us, we mark our forehead with the sign of the cross" (*On the Soldier's Crown*).

C. **Cyril of Jerusalem** wrote in the middle of the fourth century: "Let us not be ashamed to confess the Crucified. Let the Cross, as our seal, be boldly made with our fingers upon our brow, and on all occasions; over the bread we eat, over the cups we drink; in our comings and in our goings; before sleep; on lying down and rising up; when we are on the way and when we are still" (*Catechesis* 13, ch. 36).

D. **Martin Luther**, the father of the Protestant Reformation, in his catechism also encouraged making the sign of the cross: "In the morning, when you get up, make the sign of the holy cross and say: In the name of the Father and of the Son and of the Holy Ghost. Amen." "In the evening, when you go to bed, make the sign of the holy cross and say. . . ." (*Luther's Small Catechism*, Section 2).

E. The sign of the cross was most strongly opposed by the small sect of the Puritans in England during the late 1500s. Influenced by John Calvin, they rejected as superstitious and idolatrous the use of any symbols not expressly prescribed in Scripture. This included not only the sign of the cross, but vestments, candles, and even organs. It was these Puritans who formed a significant part of the early colonists in America.

II. The cross is the central symbol of the Christian Faith and by tracing its shape upon ourselves we declare that we belong to Jesus Christ.

A. **Our Lord Himself spoke of the cross symbolically**, even before His own crucifixion:

1. "If anyone desires to come after Me, let him deny himself, and **take up his cross daily**, and follow Me" (Luke 9:23; see also Matthew 16:24 and Mark 8:34).

2. "**Whoever does not bear his cross** and come after Me cannot be My disciple" (Luke 14:27; see also Matthew 10:38 and Mark 10:21).

B. **Our Lord voluntarily died on a cross** to bring us redemption from sin and victory over death and Satan. This is the primary reason the cross became a precious symbol for all Christians.

C. **Paul the Apostle spoke of the cross** in this way: "May it never be that I should boast, except in the cross of our Lord Jesus Christ, through which the world has been crucified to me and I to the world" (Galatians 6:14 NASV).

D. There are other common gestures of the hand used in American culture to express symbolic meaning. For example: the Boy Scout sign and a military salute.

Conclusion: If it is appropriate to use this symbol on Christian books and buildings, then why can't Christians make the sign of the cross on themselves, as soldiers do a salute, to show that they belong to Christ and His army?

III. When accompanied by faith in Christ, the sign of the cross has power over sin, death, and Satan.

A. **Cyril of Jerusalem**, in the same Catechism quoted above, continued, "It is a powerful safeguard. . . . it is a grace from God, a badge of the faithful, and a terror to devils. . . . For when they see the Cross, they are reminded of the Crucified; they fear Him who has 'smashed the heads of the dragons.' Despise not the seal as a free gift, but rather for this reason honor your Benefactor all the more" (*Catechesis* 13, ch. 36).

B. **Athanasius**, Bishop of Alexandria around A.D. 320, wrote a famous treatise entitled *On the Incarnation*. There he included several comments on the use of the sign of the cross.

1. "All the disciples of Christ despise death; they take the offensive against it and, instead of fearing it, by the sign of the cross and by faith in Christ trample on it as on something dead" (ch. 5, § 27).

2. "By the sign of the cross . . . all magic is stayed, all sorcery confounded, all the idols are abandoned and deserted, and all senseless pleasure ceases, as the eye of faith looks up from earth to heaven" (ch. 5, § 31).

3. ". . . by the sign of the cross, if a man will use it, he drives out the deceits of demons" (ch. 8, § 47).

C. **John Chrysostom**, at the end of the fourth century, wrote: "The Sign of the Cross is the type of our deliverance, the monument of liberation of mankind, the souvenir of the forbearance of Our Lord. When you make it, remember what has been given for your ransom, and you will be the slave of no one. Make it, then, not only with the fingers, but with your faith. If you engrave it on your forehead, no impure spirit will dare to stand before you. He sees the blade with which he has been wounded, and the sword with which he has received the deathblow."

Conclusion: The true power of the cross is exhibited in accordance with our faith in Christ and our true willingness to deny ourselves and follow Him. Like Him, we must be willing to accept, if necessary, suffering, shame, and death, for the sake of God. Those who use the sign of the cross superstitiously do not understand the true meaning of the cross.

In summary to the question of why we use the sign of the cross, it might be helpful to comment on how and when it can be made.

1. It appears that in the earliest centuries Christians simply traced the form of the cross on their foreheads with either the index finger or the thumb of their right hand.

2. By the 700s the custom had arisen which is still the practice of Orthodox Christians today. The thumb, the index finger, and the middle finger of the right hand are joined together (this was seen as a picture of the Trinity). The other two fingers are bent down to the palm (this was seen as a picture of the two natures in Christ). The cross is then traced by touching the three fingers to the forehead, the chest, the right shoulder and then the left shoulder (this shows we have given ourselves to God with all our mind, our heart, and our strength [cf. Luke 10:27]).

3. Around the year 1200, Christians in the Roman Catholic Church began making the sign of the cross with all their fingers extended and going from the forehead, to the chest, to the left shoulder and then to the right (see *The Byzantine-Slav Liturgy of St. John Chrysostom*, by Kucharek, pp. 339–40.)

However the sign of the cross is made, though, the meaning of the cross remains the same. In the words of one present-day monk: "When we make the sign of the cross we are crossing out ourselves and saying, 'not my way God, but Yours'; not 'glory to me,' but 'glory to the Father and to the Son and to the Holy Spirit, now and ever and unto ages of ages. Amen.' "

See also the articles "The Sign of the Cross, Its Meaning and Origins," *by Fr. Jack Sparks, and* "The Cross, A Sign for All Christians," *by Fr. Weldon Hardenbrook, published in* Again Magazine *Vol. 6, No. 1.*

Q. Why do we use church tradition as a source for our beliefs and practices and not the Bible alone as many Protestants claim is proper?

A. Because the Bible commands us to be faithful to the tradition of the Apostles; and the Bible cannot be (nor does it claim to be) a self-sufficient source of Christian belief and practice. Furthermore all Christians rely on church tradition to some degree, whether they are aware of it or not. The real question, then, is not whether or not to rely on tradition, but on *which* tradition to rely, the tradition of men or the Holy Tradition of the Apostles, which has been preserved and kept by the Church.

I. The Bible commands us to be faithful to the tradition of the Apostles.

A. **1 Corinthians 11:2**—"Now I praise you, brethren, that you remember me in all things and **keep the traditions** [Greek *paradóseis*] **just as I delivered them to you.**"

B. **1 Corinthians 15:3**—"For I delivered [Greek *parédoka*—same Greek root as above] to you first of all that which I also received." (See also 1 Corinthians 11:23.)

C. **2 Thessalonians 2:15**—"Therefore, brethren, stand fast and **hold the traditions** [Greek *paradóseis*] **which you were taught, whether by word or our epistle.**" (See also 2 Thessalonians 3:6.)

D. **2 Timothy 2:2**—"And the things that you have heard from me among many witnesses, commit these to faithful men who will be able to teach others also."

E. **The Greek word for tradition is *parádosis*. It means literally something handed down or delivered over.** In the New Testament texts quoted above it refers to the body of truth (including both beliefs and practices) that Jesus Christ delivered to the Apostles (both by His preaching and by His example), which they in turn delivered to the churches made up of those who believed in Jesus Christ through their teaching. **This body of truth was at first solely oral tradition and only began to be written down twenty to sixty years later in the Gospels of the New Testament.**

II. The Bible cannot be (nor does it claim to be) a self-sufficient source of Christian belief and practice.

A. **The Bible does not contain all that Christ said and did.** St. John the Evangelist wrote: "And there are also many other things that Jesus did, which if they were written one by one, I suppose that even the world itself could not contain the books that would be written" (John 21:25).

B. **The early Christians had nothing like the Bible as we know it today, yet it would be foolish to imagine that they were lacking in either beliefs or practices.** Their faith was founded on the tradition which they had received from the Apostles and which they had faithfully preserved and kept just as St. Paul had directed.

C. **The Bible can be understood differently by different people.** If it were meant to have been self-sufficient, this would not be the case.

   1. 2 Peter 1:20—"But know this first of all, that **no prophecy of Scripture is a matter of one's own interpretation**" (NASV).

   2. 2 Peter 3:15, 16—". . . our beloved brother Paul, according to the wisdom given to him, has written to you, as also in all his epistles, speaking in them of these things, **in which are some things hard to understand,** which untaught and unstable people twist to their own destruction, as *they do* also the rest of the Scriptures."

   3. **One of the most important roles of church tradition is to guide the interpretation of the Bible.** St. Paul spoke of the Church itself as the "the pillar and ground of the truth" (1 Timothy 3:15).

Conclusion: The Bible should be seen not as something outside of the Church's tradition, but *as part of it*. It is the infallible Word of God, to be sure, and it gives us the very words of Christ and the Apostles. As such, it has a pre-eminent and chief place within the Church's tradition and no other part of tradition can be directly opposed to it in any way. Yet at the same time, the Bible cannot be isolated from the Church and its tradition, but rather must be contained within it and completed by it.

III. All Christians rely on church tradition to some degree, whether they are aware of it or not.

A. **All Christians are dependent on church tradition to tell them which books make up the New Testament and which do not.**

    1. The Bible did not just float down out of heaven one day in a gold-edged, leather-bound, cross-referenced edition, all arranged and ready to go.

    2. The canon of the New Testament, that is, the official list of books that make up its very contents, was determined by the tradition of the early Church.

        a. St. Athanasius (around A.D. 350) was the first church leader to list as approved, "canonical" Scriptures the exact twenty-seven books we know today as the New Testament.

        b. In some regions, the divine inspiration of the Book of Revelation, the Book of Hebrews, and a few of the other, shorter epistles was not fully accepted for several hundred years. In addition, a few churches considered some books as Scripture which later were rejected.

        c. **It was not until the Third Council of Carthage in A.D. 397 that this same list we know today was first officially adopted and began the process of being firmly accepted by all Christians.**

B. **All Christians are indebted to church tradition for many things which cannot be found in the Bible**, but which they readily accept and would feel shortchanged without.

    1. Church tradition, for example, not the Bible, has established **Sunday as the day of Christian worship**, and this is accepted by virtually all Christians (except for the Seventh Day Adventists and a small number of other groups).

    2. Christ commanded the Apostles to baptize, but **the service for baptism** is not described in the Bible. It is, however, found in the Church's tradition. (The same thing can be said about the service of worship centering around the Lord's Supper.)

3. Even such an accepted thing as a "traditional" Protestant wedding ("Dearly beloved, we are gathered here today in the sight of God and these witnesses to join . . .") is part of some church tradition. This service is not outlined in the Bible, and yet many Protestant Christians have a deep and religious affection for it.

IV. The real question is *not* tradition or no tradition, but rather *which* tradition—the tradition of men or the Holy Tradition of the Apostles, which has been preserved and kept by the Church.

A. Jesus Christ strictly warned His disciples about the unholy tradition of men when He condemned the Pharisees, saying, "For laying aside the commandment of God, **you hold the tradition of men**—the washing of pitchers and cups, and many other such things . . . **making the word of God of no effect**" (Mark 7:8,13).

B. St. Paul warned likewise: "**Beware lest anyone cheat you through philosophy and empty deceit, according to the tradition of men**, according to the basic principles of the world, and not according to Christ" (Colossians 2:8).

C. The Holy Tradition of the Church, which in the earliest centuries was preserved by oral transmission, took written form in chiefly five ways:

1. The Gospels and Epistles of the New Testament.
2. The creeds and canons of the Ecumenical Councils.
3. The service books of the Church.
4. The writings of the Church Fathers.
5. The biographies of the saints.

In summary, it must be understood that tradition, like Scripture, cannot be something "dusty," but must be alive. This is well phrased by one contemporary Orthodox monk in a booklet entitled *Tradition in the Church*:

"Holy tradition is the sum and substance, the fundamental and essential coherence and unity of the sacred books of the Bible. It is not a deposit of doctrine learned by heart, but a way of life, the way of holiness (Isaiah 35:8). It is not the sum of past experience, but a living experience of God's action today. It is not a dead dependence on the past, but a living and total dependence on the Holy Spirit."

Holy Tradition is the footprint of the Holy Spirit in the history of the Church. It is the fulfillment of Christ's promise to His disciples: "The Helper, the Holy Spirit, whom the Father will send in My name, He will teach you all things, and bring to your remembrance all things that I said to you" (John 14:26).

Q. Why do we venerate icons when the Ten Commandments read: "You shall not make for yourself a carved image. . . . you shall not bow down to them nor serve them" (Exodus 20:4, 5)?

A. Because the purpose of this commandment was to keep Israel from falling into idolatry, not to forbid the use of all images.

The Orthodox use of icons is important for several reasons:
1. icons help safeguard the right belief about Jesus Christ;
2. icons are a visual aid for teaching the Christian Faith;
3. icons help us remember the Christians in ages past;
4. icons can help communicate to us the reality of the presence of God and the heavenly realm in our daily lives.

The use and veneration of icons is an ancient Christian

> tradition that was upheld by the Seventh Ecumenical Council held in Nicaea in A.D. 787. This Council explained that the veneration Christians show to icons is a sign of honor and reverence directed to the person or event depicted and not to the material of the icon itself. Furthermore, the Church has always maintained a strict distinction between this kind of honor or reverence and the worship due to God alone.

I. The purpose of the second commandment was to keep Israel from falling into idolatry, not to forbid the use of all images.

A. Israel was surrounded by many peoples who worshipped manmade idols as gods and had to be specifically warned about adopting their ways.

B. The first commandment explains the purpose of the second: **"You shall have no other gods before Me"** (Exodus 20:3).

C. The conclusion of the second commandment also explains its purpose: "For I, the LORD your God, *am* a jealous God" (Exodus 20:5).

D. Moses told Israel that God could not be depicted in an image because He did not have material form: "Take careful heed to yourselves, for **you saw no form when the LORD spoke to you at Horeb out of the midst of the fire**, lest you act corruptly and make for yourselves a carved image in the form of any figure" (Deuteronomy 4:15).

E. **God elsewhere commanded Israel to make certain images and use them in their worship.**

1. **Exodus 25:18**—"You shall make two cherubim of gold."

2. **Exodus 26:1**—"You shall make the tabernacle *with* ten curtains *of* fine woven linen, and blue, purple, and scarlet thread; **with artistic designs of cherubim you shall weave them.**"

3. **Numbers 21:8**—"**Make a fiery** *serpent*, **and set it on a pole.**"

4. **1 Kings 6:29**—"Then [Solomon] carved all the walls of the temple all around, both the inner and outer *sanctuaries*, **with carved figures of cherubim, palm trees, and open flowers.**"

5. **Ezekiel 41:25**—**"Cherubim and palm trees *were* carved on the doors of the temple just as they *were* carved on the walls"** (from Ezekiel's vision of the temple in heaven).

Conclusion—Icons are in no way like idols. They do not attempt to depict the divine nature of God and they do not detract from the worship that is due to God alone. Therefore the second commandment given by Moses to Israel is not relevant to the Church's use of icons.

II. The Orthodox use of icons is important for several reasons:

A. Icons help safeguard the right belief about Jesus Christ.

1. An icon of Jesus Christ declares that He really was and still is a human being with a form like ours.
    a. At various times different people have taught that the material world is evil and that therefore the divine Son of God did not become a real man, or else He was somehow not the same person as the human Jesus. Such people opposed any icons of Christ.
    b. By declaring that Jesus Christ still bears real, material human form, icons help maintain the attitude Christians should have toward the material world, namely that it is *not* intrinsically evil.

2. When we see an icon of Jesus Christ and confess that this man is also truly and fully God, the mystery and wonder of His coming in the flesh is made plain.

3. The icons of Mary, the Mother of God, are also primarily intended to declare this same mystery of the Incarnation.

B. Icons are visual aids for teaching the Christian Faith.

1. **St. John of Damascus** wrote: "Icons are the books of the illiterate, the never silent heralds of the honor due the saints, teaching without use of words those who gaze upon them, and sanctifying the sense of sight. Suppose I have few books, or little leisure for reading, but walk into the spiritual hospital—that is to say, a church—with my soul choking from the prickles of thorny thoughts, and thus afflicted I see before me the brilliance of the icon. I am refreshed as if in a lush meadow, and thus my soul is led to glorify God" (*On the Divine Images*, St. Vladimir's Seminary Press, p. 39).

C. Icons help us remember the Christians in ages past.

1. Icons of the saints are also like the "family photos" of the Church,

pictures of our loved ones whose victories in the Christian life encourage us and provide an example for us.

2. No one should object to icons used in this way who finds no fault in displaying the pictures of relatives, or the presidents of the United States, or the past heads of colleges, or any heroes whom they admire and wish to emulate.

D. Icons can help communicate to us the reality of the presence of God and the heavenly realm in our daily lives.
1. Images do have the power to communicate.
   a. Advertising agencies know and exploit this power through their use of famous personalities, social symbols, and product logos.
   b. The Soviet Union used this power in hanging portraits of Lenin everywhere in public so that he could continue to influence society even though he had been dead since 1924. (Communist China does the same thing with portraits of Mao.)
   c. Nearly everyone can testify to the strong emotions different symbols can arouse, such as a swastika, an American flag, a peace sign, or a Coca-Cola logo.
   d. A soldier who carries a portrait of his wife and children in his pocket and perhaps sometimes even kisses it feels that this image communicates to him something of the reality of his family.
2. Likewise, there can be a similar power in icons, namely the power to communicate something of the essence of the person depicted.
   a. St. John of Damascus wrote: "By itself matter [e.g. wood, paint, etc.] deserves no worship, but if someone portrayed in an image is full of grace, we become partakers of the grace **according to the measure of our faith**" (*On the Divine Images*, St. Vladimir's Seminary Press, p. 37).
   b. For this reason, icons are sometimes referred to as "windows to heaven" or "thin-places," that is, places where our present earthly realm and the realm of heaven are brought close together.
   c. Also in this regard one should consider the various miracles that are reported to have been accomplished through some icons.

Conclusion—Icons, therefore, can communicate some sense of the presence of the person depicted, even if only to a small degree. As St. John of Damascus wrote, this is dependent upon the faith of the person. (For this reason Orthodox Christians are often said to pray not "to" icons but "before" icons. The only One we can pray *to*, of course, is God.)

III. The use and veneration of icons is an ancient Christian tradition that was upheld by the Seventh Ecumenical Council held in Nicaea in A.D. 787.

A. The word "icon" comes from the Greek word *eikon*, meaning "image."

B. Christians in the first century used the symbols of a dove, a fish, and a shepherd as simple religious art.

C. Pictorial representations of events in the life of Christ can be found in the catacombs of Rome and Alexandria dating from the early 100s.

D. By the fourth century, there are many Christian writers bearing witness to the powerful role icons held in the Church. These include St. Basil, St. John Chrysostom, and St. Athanasius.

E. The seventh and last Ecumenical Council met in the year A.D. 787 specifically to answer the question of whether or not it was proper for Christians to venerate icons. This ancient custom was being opposed at that time by a movement started by the Byzantine Emperor Leo the Isaurian. The decree of the Council, which was signed unanimously by the 350 bishops present, reads:

> "To make our confession short, we keep unchanged all the ecclesiastical traditions handed down to us, whether in writing or verbally, **one of which is the making of pictorial representations, agreeable to the history of preaching the Gospel, a tradition useful in many respects**, but especially in this, that the incarnation of the Word of God is shown forth as real and not merely phantom-like. . . . **The venerable and holy images (icons) in painting and mosaic as well as other fitting materials should be set forth in the holy churches of God . . . in houses and by the wayside.** . . . For by so much more frequently as they are seen in artistic representation, by so much more readily are men lifted up to the memory of their prototypes, and to long after them" (*Nicene and Post-Nicene Fathers,* Vol. XIV, p. 550).

IV. The veneration Christians show to icons is a sign of honor and reverence directed to the person or event depicted and not to the material of the icon itself. Furthermore, the Church has always maintained a strict distinction between this kind of honor or reverence and the worship due to God alone.

A. The decree of the Seventh Ecumenical Council continues, saying: "**To these [icons] should be given due salutation and honorable reverence** [Greek *aspasmón kai timetekén proskúnesin*], not indeed the true worship of faith [Greek *latréian*] which pertains alone to the divine nature; but to these, as to the figure of the life-giving Cross and to the Book of the Gospel and to other holy objects, incense and candles may be offered according to ancient pious custom. **For honor which is paid to the image passes on to that which the image represents, and he who reveres the image reveres in it the subject represented**" (op. cit., p. 550).

1. Note that the Greek Church Fathers reserved the word *latréia* for the worship that is due to God alone. This is the word that forms the root of the suffix "-latry" in words such as "idolatry" (see Matthew 4:10).

2. The Greek word *proskúnesin* is a more general term for honor and is used in various ways even in the Bible (see Hebrews 11:21).

3. When we venerate the icon of St. John the Evangelist, for example, we are not honoring or reverencing the material of the icon, but St. John himself. This is the meaning of the last statement quoted above.

B. Those who might protest the veneration of icons, which is commonly expressed by kissing them, show veneration for other things by similar physical gestures.

1. For example, all Americans are used to saluting the flag or taking off their hats during the national anthem. This is a form of veneration.

2. Most Protestant Christians venerate the Bible highly and many will not set another book on top of it or treat it disrespectfully by tossing it around. This also is a form of veneration.

Conclusion—If it is acceptable to honor a flag, which is made of fabric and dye, or a book, which is made of paper and ink, then it also should be acceptable to honor the images of Christ and His saints, which are made of wood and paint. For it should be clear to everyone that we are not really honoring fabric or paper or wood, but the things which these have been made to symbolize.

> *Q.* Why do we have an established organization and structure in our Church when some Christians see this as a corruption of the "Spirit-filled church of Acts" into a manmade institution?
>
> *A.* The simple answer is because the "Spirit-filled church of Acts" also had an established organization and structure, and those who fail to recognize this and assume that organization and structure are automatically a sign of corruption are mistaken. From the teaching of the Bible as well as from the experience of history, it is evident that the Church has two dimensions which must function together: its structural and organizational dimension, and its spiritual and charismatic dimension.

I. The "Spirit-filled church of Acts" had an established organization and structure.

A. Our Lord showed organization when He selected twelve men from among His many followers to be His disciples and the founders of His Church.

1. "You did not choose Me, but **I chose you and appointed you** that you should go and bear fruit" (John 15:16).

2. **Jesus established Peter as the head of the twelve**: "you are Peter, and on this rock I will build My church ... And I will give you the keys of the kingdom of heaven" (Matthew 16:18, 19).

B. Organization and structure were also part of the Church in Acts.
   1. **Peter continued to be recognized as the head of the Twelve and the early Church** (see Acts 1:15; 2:14; and 5:3).
   2. **The Apostles felt it was imperative to elect someone to fill the apostolic "office" left vacant by the death of Judas, so Matthias was chosen** (Acts 1:15–26).
   3. **The Apostles ordained seven deacons to help in the practical administration and organization of the church in Jerusalem.**
      a. The twelve Apostles put forth the conditions for their election: "Seek out from among you seven men of *good* reputation, full of the Holy Spirit and wisdom" (Acts 6:3).
      b. The congregation of the church made the choice (Acts 6:5).
      c. The twelve Apostles then laid hands on them that they might receive the authority and spiritual gifting to perform their service (Acts 6:6).
      d. This procedure became the pattern that the Orthodox Church has used ever since in appointing its leadership.
   4. **The church council described in Acts 15 was an appeal to the authority of the organized leadership of the church in Jerusalem**, and its decision was then announced by letter to the Gentile Christians in Antioch, Syria, and Cilicia.
   5. **The Apostles appointed elders** [Greek *presbyters*] **to rule the new churches they raised up** (Acts 14:23) **and instructed the people to obey them** (Hebrews 13:17 and 1 Peter 5:5).
   6. The beliefs of the early churches strictly followed the doctrines and practices approved by the Apostles and elders in Jerusalem.
      a. "And they continued steadfastly in the apostles' doctrine and fellowship, in the breaking of bread, and in prayers" (Acts 2:42).
      b. **"And as they went through the cities, they delivered to them the decrees to keep, which were determined by the apostles and elders at Jerusalem"** (Acts 16:4).
   7. There was coordination among the churches in different cities and a sense of responsibility one to another, as seen in the missionary journeys of Paul (Acts 13:3) and the aid sent to Jerusalem in the time of famine (Acts 11:29).

8. Peter's description of the Church in his first epistle assumes some sort of organization and structure: ". . . **you *are* a chosen generation, a royal priesthood, a holy nation**" (1 Peter 2:9).

C. The writings of the apostolic fathers show that the Church at the end of the first century had definite organization and structure.

1. Clement, Bishop of Rome in A.D. 95, wrote in a letter to the church in Corinth: "as [the Apostles] preached from country to country and from city to city, they appointed their first converts, after testing them by the Spirit, to be the bishops and deacons of the future believers. Nor was this an innovation; since bishops and deacons had been written of long before" (*First Clement* 42:4, 5).

2. Ignatius, Bishop of Antioch from A.D. 69 until his martyrdom under Trajan in the second century, wrote: "All of you are to follow the bishop as Jesus Christ follows the Father, and the presbytery as the apostles. Respect the deacons as the command of God. Apart from the bishop no one is to do anything pertaining to the church" (*Epistle to the Smyrnaeans* 8).

Conclusion—Those who would like to blame a supposed "manmade institutionalism" for the faults they find in the later life of the Church should realize that all the elements of later church organization and structure were also present in the Church of Acts in a simple and seedlike form. There was official leadership on both the local and Church-wide level; organized, authoritative councils; an approved form of belief and practice; and a network of interaction between churches. It is true that these elements matured and further developed as the Church itself became larger and more complex. But this was not corruption or invention. It was only the natural and necessary maturing of an order already in existence.

II. The Church has two dimensions which must function together:

A. A **structural and organizational dimension** is necessary.

1. This includes such things as government, administration, regulations, traditions, and customs, as discussed above.

2. Without this, the Church becomes individualistic and therefore open to fanaticism, heresy, division, and—occasionally—outright weirdness.

B. A **spiritual and charismatic dimension** is necessary.

1. This refers to the direct work of the Holy Spirit within the Church through various gifts and callings (1 Corinthians 12:4–11); or through

miraculous experiences, such as the conversion of Paul (Acts 9), or the vision of Peter (Acts 10).

2. Without this, the Church becomes bound up with authority, law, and tradition; the leadership and people become separated from each other; superstition replaces faith; and formalism suffocates the Holy Spirit.

C. These two dimensions in church life can be seen in several biblical illustrations.

1. Jesus described the Gospel as **new wine needing a new wineskin** (Matthew 9:17). The wineskin can be understood as the structural dimension of the Church and the wine as the spiritual dimension.

2. Jesus also used the illustration of the Gospel as **yeast and dough**, which can be understood in a similar way (Matthew 13:33).

3. Paul referred to **the Church as the body of Christ** (Ephesians 1:22, 23 and Colossians 1:18).
   a. A healthy body is obviously a complex organism with one head and many different parts functioning in order and harmony.
   b. But it is the spirit within the body that gives it life and direction.

D. **For the Church to function properly as the new wine and new wineskin, as the body of Christ, its structural and organizational dimension must always be a servant to its spiritual and charismatic dimension.**

1. The form and organization of the Church is a container to be filled with the life of the Holy Spirit (Ephesians 2:21, 22).

2. This is the way God has chosen to work among men in our world: "My strength is made perfect in weakness" (2 Corinthians 12:9).

3. When the organization of the Church begins to dominate or the life of the Spirit is suppressed, the Church can indeed become a lifeless and man-made institution.

4. Such imbalances have occurred in the history of the Church, but it would be naive and wrongheaded to try therefore to dispose with all forms of church organization or structure. (It would be another classic case of "throwing the baby out with the bathwater.")

5. God has always worked in the Church to bring about spiritual renewal and restore its higher, spiritual dimension. (Consider, for example, the rise and influence of monasticism.)

E. **Conclusion**: Fr. Alexander Schmemann summarizes these things well in his book *Historical Road of Eastern Orthodoxy*:

> "The [early church] community has often been contrasted with the 'organized' Church of a later age, as though early Christians had been a kind of fluid, ecstatic brotherhood living on inspiration, with no authority except the 'breath of the Spirit.' In fact, however, from the beginning the very concept of a Church included the idea of an organized society, and nothing was more foreign to the early Christian outlook than any kind of opposition between spirit and form, or between freedom and organization. Human society, they believed, was now filled with the Spirit of God and was thereby a vehicle of the divine life, so that everything human in society becomes a channel for things divine, while everything spiritual is made incarnate in the life of mankind" (St. Vladimir's Seminary Press, 1977, pp. 12, 13).

Other Small Booklets Available from Conciliar Press:

What Is the Orthodox Church?
by Fr. Marc Dunaway
A brief overview of Orthodoxy. Outlines the history of the Christian Church, with concise explanations and helpful "at-a-glance" timelines. Includes the Age of Persecution, the Age of Councils, the Great Schism, the Protestant Reformation, and more.
24-page booklet—Order No. 000203—$2.95

Orthodoxy and Catholicism: What Are the Differences?
by Fr. Theodore Pulcini
A former Roman Catholic chronicles his own journey into Orthodoxy and examines the critical issues that influenced his decision, including papal authority, the *filioque* controversy, and the "new" dogmas.
24-page booklet—Order No. 000266—$3.50

Sola Scriptura
by Fr. John Whiteford
An Orthodox analysis of a Protestant bastion: private interpretation of Scripture. Exposes the fallacies on which this doctrine is based and explains the Orthodox approach to Holy Scripture.
47-page booklet (ISBN 1-888212-04-7)—Order No. 001983—$3.95

Apostolic Succession
by Fr. Gregory Rogers
Examines the unbroken apostolic chain linking past to present in the historic Church. Written by a former evangelical pastor whose study of the biblical and historical evidence supporting this very doctrine led him to the two-thousand-year-old Orthodox Church.
42-page booklet (ISBN 0-9622713-7-3)—Order No. 000026—$3.95

Bodily Resurrection
By the Sisters of the Orthodox Monastery of the Transfiguration
Explains the Orthodox understanding of the body, death, and resurrection and presents a compelling apologetic for burial (as opposed to cremation) as an affirmation of our expectation of eternal life.
32-page booklet (ISBN 1-888212-10-1)—Order No. 003097—$2.95

To request a Conciliar Press catalog of introductory books about the Orthodox Faith and Church life, to place a credit card order, or to obtain current ordering information, please call Conciliar Press at (800) 967-7377 or (831) 336-5118, or log on to our website: www.conciliarpress.com